DUCKS!

A MY INCREDIBLE WORLD PICTURE BOOK

MY INCREDIBLE WORLD

Photo Credits:
Page 1. By Milada Vigerova, available at https://unsplash.com/photos/Qf3j1lHfyik
Page 2. Bu Håkon Helberg, available at https://unsplash.com/photos/8qxzIaf6-j0
Page 3. By Dennis Buchner, available at https://unsplash.com/photos/FwRVS2mleWg
Page 4. By Gary Bendig, available at https://unsplash.com/photos/5x7PrmmHanG4
Page 5. By Matt Silveria, available at https://unsplash.com/photos/gevel6AKpGU
Page 6. "Duck" by Filip Stepien, available at https://www.flickr.com/photos/150203417@N08/34412412640. licensed under CC BY 2.0. (Full terms at https://creativecommons.org/licenses/by/2.0.)
Page 7. By MabelAmber, available at https://pixabay.com/en/duck-mallard-drake-bird-water-bird-3319107
Page 8. By Ben Pattinson, available at https://unsplash.com/photos/_Wo1Oq38fVU
Page 9. By Ravi Singh, available at https://unsplash.com/photos/rN3dqzDrhdk
Page 10. By Benny Jackson, available at https://unsplash.com/photos/NANw4EPI0Yk
Page 11. By Joe Cox, available at https://unsplash.com/photos/7yObxohaj-k
Page 12. By Roksolana Zasiadko, available at https://unsplash.com/photos/JVu3_fQ_7Ek
Page 13. By Jorge Alcala, available at https://unsplash.com/photos/EPLK3AWORjM
Page 14. By Ray Hennessy, available at https://unsplash.com/photos/yQZgEb4u-Dw
Page 15. By Ryk Naves, available at https://unsplash.com/photos/XJOyOmp0Hzc
Page 16. By Lindz Marsh, available at https://unsplash.com/photos/cfFbdoh3EVo
Page 17. By Vincent van Zalinge, available at https://unsplash.com/photos/MM2bY4W7G2Y
Page 18. By Josh Appel, available at https://unsplash.com/photos/a8XPFiACGP4
Page 19. By Val Vesa, available at https://unsplash.com/photos/W1Euyq5oDS8
Page 20. By Dennis Buchner, available at https://unsplash.com/photos/WATeNJyEUkA
Page 21. By Robert Szadkowski, available at https://unsplash.com/photos/b7nK3aECcRI
Page 22. By Capri23auto, available at https://pixabay.com/en/violet-duck-small-mountain-duck-duck-3347336

Ducks are mostly aquatic birds that live in both fresh and sea water.

Ducks are found on every continent in the world except Antarctica.

There are many different species of ducks.

Some ducks are wild and some live
on farms or as pets.

Ducks are omnivores, eating mostly plants, bugs, worms, grubs and slugs!

The most common and recognizable wild duck in the U.S. is the Mallard.

Mallards, a kind of dabbling duck, dip headfirst into the water to find food!

Most ducks grow to be around
20 to 26 inches long.

Adult ducks usually weigh between 1.6 and 3.5 pounds.

A male duck is called a drake.

A female duck is called a hen or a duck.

Baby ducks are called ducklings.

Ducks rely more on sight than any other sense.

Ducks have webbed feet that help them paddle through water!

Ducks' outer feathers are waterproof!

Ducks usually live to be
5 to 10 years old.

Ducks migrate south for the winter.

Ducks communicate using a wide variety of noises and calls!

Female mallards make the classic "quack" sound, but males do not!

Ducks can sleep with one eye open!

A group of ducks on water is called a raft, a team or a paddling.

Ducks are incredible!